First Number Book

KING*f*ISHER

KINGFISHER
Kingfisher Publications Plc
New Penderel House
283–288 High Holborn
London WC1V 7HZ
www.kingfisherpub.com

First published by Kingfisher Publications Plc 2001
First published in paperback 2002
2 4 6 8 10 9 7 5 3 1 (hb)

1RD/0302/TIMS/FR(FR)/150MA

2 4 6 8 10 9 7 5 3 1 (pb)

1TR/0302/TIMS/FR(FR)/150MA

A CIP catalogue record for this book is available from the British Library.

ISBN 0 7534 0537 1 (hb)   ISBN 0 7534 0686 1 (pb)

Printed in China

Written by Patti Barber
Illustrated by Mandy Stanley
Editors: Katie Puckett, Camilla Reid
Designer: Jane Buckley
DTP Co-ordinator: Nicky Studdart
Production: Caroline Jackson
Educational Consultant: Ann Montague-Smith

Contents

    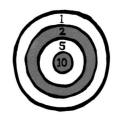

Suggestions for parents

This colourful and exciting first number book is an invaluable way for you to help your child become familiar with numbers and counting. Counting may seem straightforward to adults, but it is a complex set of concepts for children to understand. By encouraging young children to have fun with mathematics, you will help them to build confidence.

When looking at this book with your child, get him or her to guess how many things they can see around them. Talk about numbers in everyday life, for example by pointing out numbers when you are in the street. Discuss numbers that are special to your family such as telephone numbers, car numbers and ages. Children are also fascinated by halves and quarters. Look at the sizes in their clothes and shoes.

Make it interesting and exciting when you look at this book together. Ask your child to point to the objects one by one. Encourage your child to say and then learn the first few number names. Talk about the sequence of numbers – the order that they are in, ie 1,2,3,4,5. Ask what number comes next. Talk about the last number named when you are counting, and discuss how many objects there are altogether.

Encourage your child to get a feel for estimating quantities by looking at the total amount first. Then encourage him or her to learn a few more number names in order. Read stories and rhymes to practise counting backwards from 5 to 0. Use ordinal number names – ie what comes first, second, third etc.

Mathematics is not simply about numbers and counting, it also includes shape and space and measures. There are some examples of these in the book, too. 'Puppy goes for a walk' involves early language associated with space, and you can talk about journeys that you go on together. Shapes of objects are also part of mathematics and the book includes pages on straight-sided and curved-sided objects, as well as opposites such as thick and thin. Early interest in measures can be encouraged by including your child in cooking and practical tasks. And they should look at the gauges on measuring instruments such as petrol pumps, scales and rulers.

But most of all have fun!

Patti Barber

Patti Barber, Lecturer in Primary Education
Institute of Education, University of London

How many can you see?

3 houses

5 snowmen

How many windows does each house have?

4 ice creams

1 butterfly

2 dolls

Can you count all the buttons on the snowmen?

Count from 1 to 10

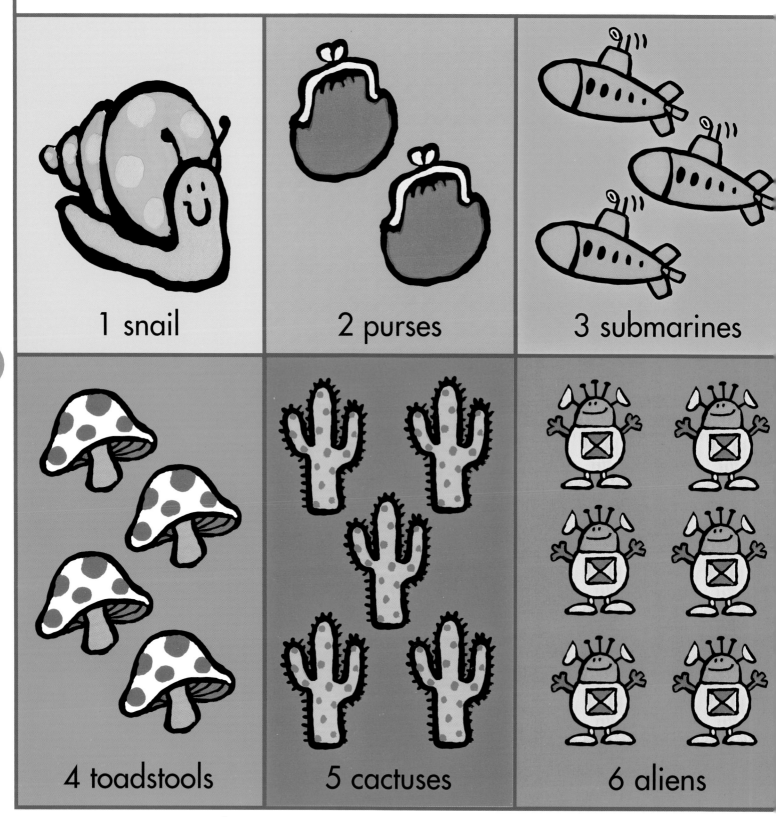

1 snail

2 purses

3 submarines

4 toadstools

5 cactuses

6 aliens

How many fingers do you have on each hand?

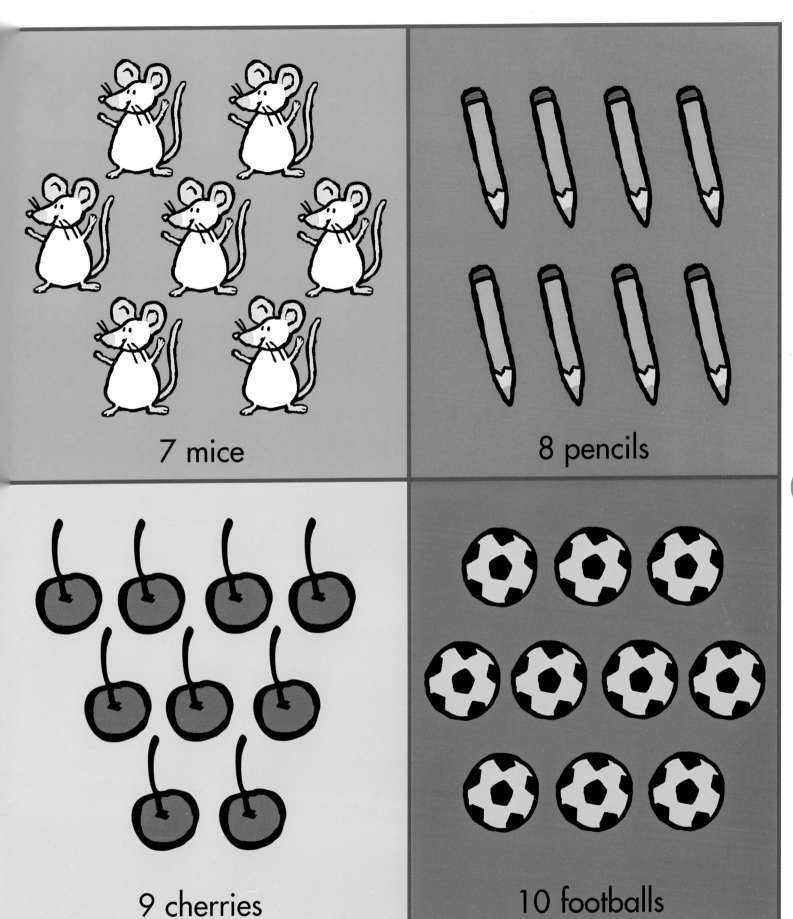

7 mice

8 pencils

9 cherries

10 footballs

How many toes do you have altogether?

Counting at the seaside

5 starfish

3 crabs

6 windmills

7 sandcastles

2 rubber rings

10

What else could you count at the seaside?

10 toes in the sand

1 ice cream van

9 buckets and spades

4 pairs of sunglasses

8 shells

What can you count in your garden?

Can you find 5?

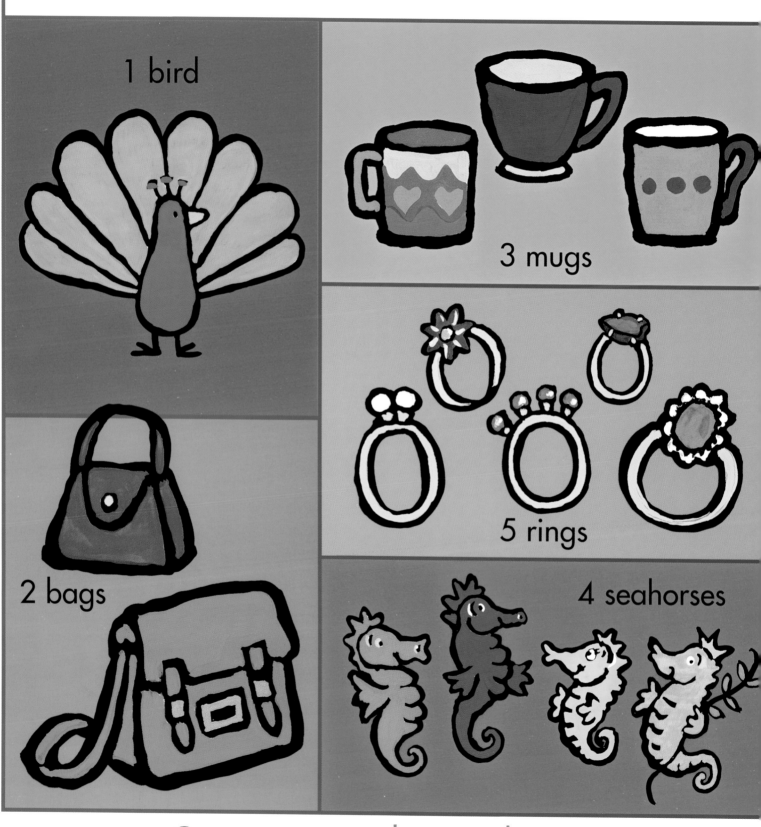

1 bird

3 mugs

5 rings

2 bags

4 seahorses

Can you spot the number 5?

5 cats

4 flowers

5

3 bugs

1 polar bear

Can you count 5 of your toys?

Who has the most babies?

The frog has 5 tadpoles.

The swan has 3 cygnets.

The rabbit has 4 bunnies.

The fox has 2 cubs.

Who has the fewest babies?

The lion has 4 cubs.

The kangaroo has 1 joey.

The pig has 2 piglets.

The hen has 3 chicks.

Does the pig have more babies than the lion?

Who is carrying the least?

The horse is carrying 2 riders.

The red clown is carrying 4 balloons.

The purple and blue clown is carrying 5 flowers.

How many are carrying 2?

The blue clown is carrying 2 pies.

The green clown is carrying 3 birds.

The yellow clown is carrying 2 buckets.

The bicycle is carrying 3 acrobats.

The seal is carrying 1 ball.

The juggler is carrying 4 clubs.

How many clowns can you see?

In what order do you get dressed?

2nd t-shirt

6th trainers

8th hat

7th jacket

4th socks

Do you get dressed in this order?

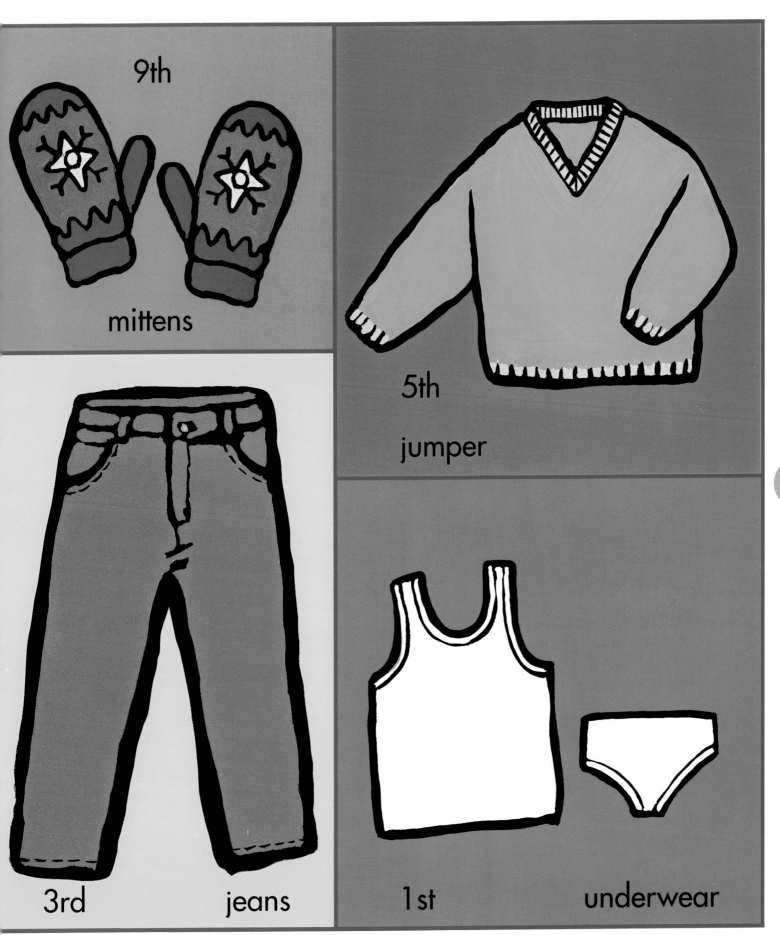

9th

mittens

5th

jumper

3rd jeans

1st underwear

19

What do you put on last?

Where does puppy go on his walk?

First, puppy goes out of the gate.

Then, he walks under the bridge.

Next, he climbs up the hill...

...and runs down the steps.

Which is the second place that puppy visits?

After that, puppy hides behind the flowers.

Then, he crosses over the river...

...and stops for a rest in front of the pond.

Puppy runs through the woods...

...scampers along the path...

...and goes into the house.

Can you count the places that puppy visits?

Count the sides on each shape

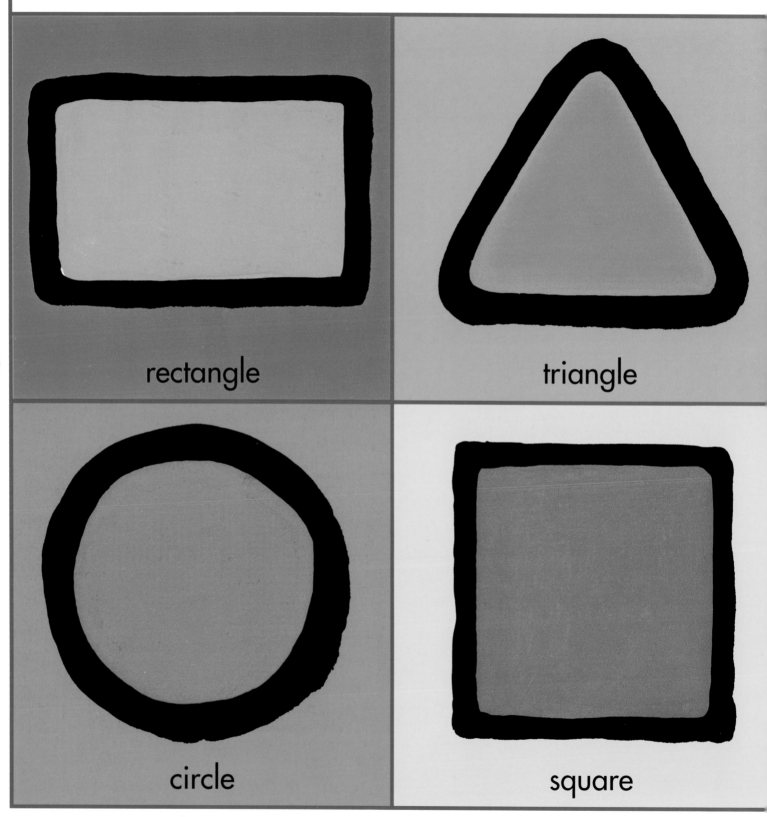

rectangle

triangle

circle

square

Which shape has the most sides?

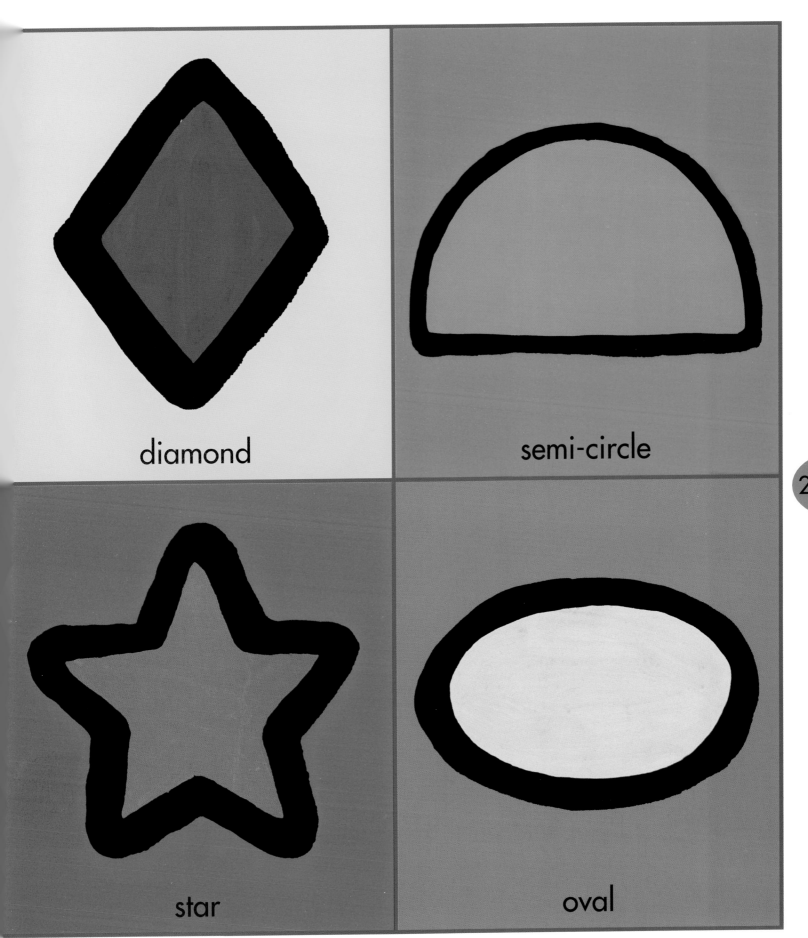

diamond

semi-circle

star

oval

Which shapes have the least sides?

Find the numbers at home

front door

target board

measuring jug

toy racing car

Are there numbers on any of your toys?

telephone

bathroom scales

cooker

envelope

Miss Sally Smith
10 Lower Street
Seatown

clock radio

12:18

What other numbers can you see in your home?

Can you see which is longer?

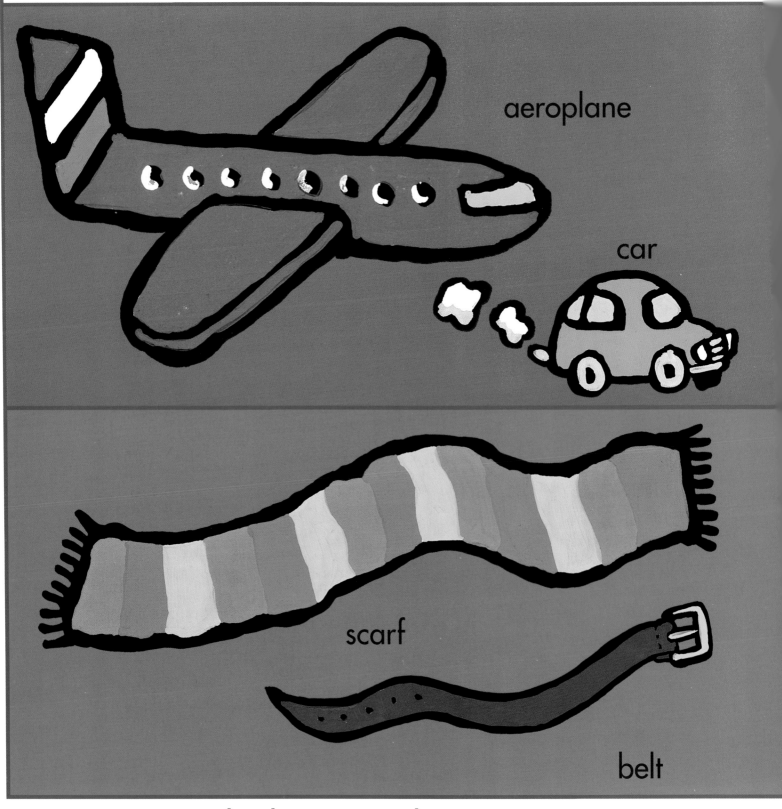

aeroplane

car

scarf

belt

Which is your longest toy?

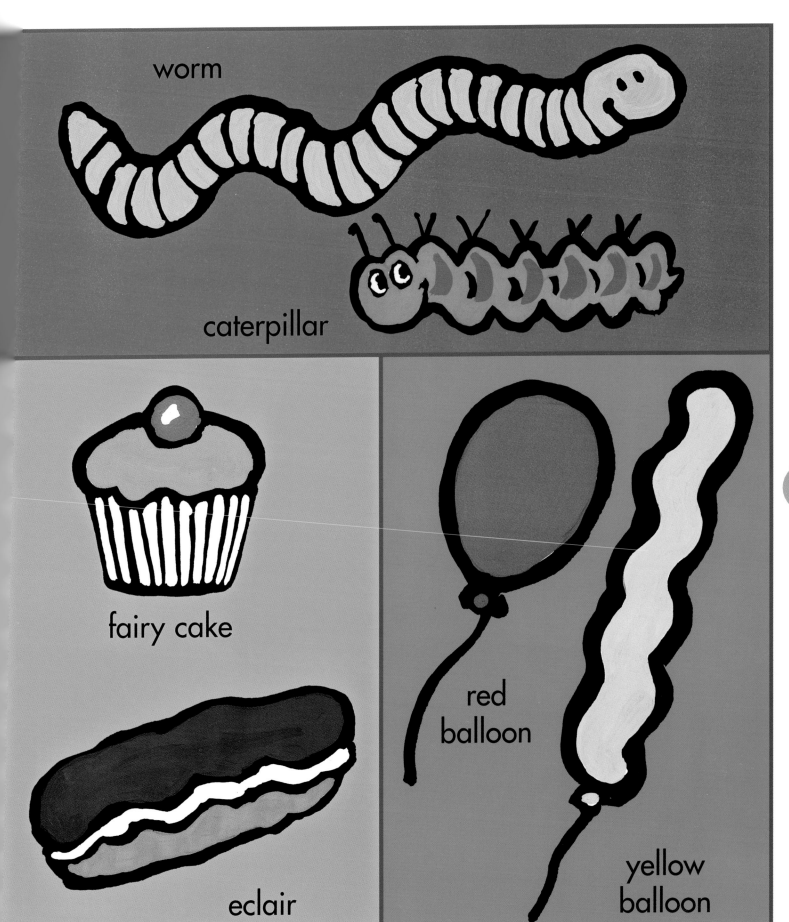

worm

caterpillar

fairy cake

eclair

red
balloon

yellow
balloon

Can you find your shortest toy?

How many animals are there?

5 penguins

1 panda

4 lemurs

3 giraffes

2 ostriches

Are there more sharks than snakes?

5 sharks

2 lions

2 camels

3 snakes

1 hippo

Are there more lions than lemurs?

Spot the opposites!

tall

short

big

small

What other opposites can you think of?

light

heavy

thick   thin

empty

full

Can you count all the things on this page?

How many wheels can you see?

train

bike

rollerskates

car

Which has the most wheels?

aeroplane

motorbike

boat

hot-air balloon

wheelchair

truck

How many have no wheels?

Are these lines curved or straight?

moon

star

dice

pear

kite

Can you see any curved lines in your home?

ladder

balls

shell

boat

umbrella

Do any of your toys have straight lines?

Are there enough for the party?

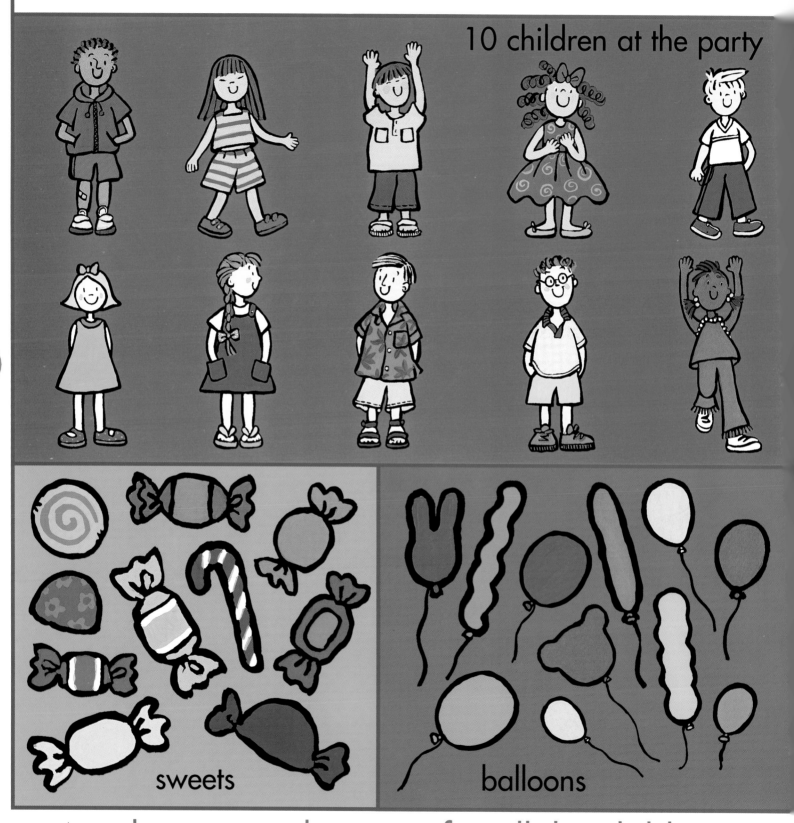

10 children at the party

sweets

balloons

Are there enough sweets for all the children?

36

cups

hats

lollies

presents

cakes

How many more cakes will be needed?

Count from 11 to 20

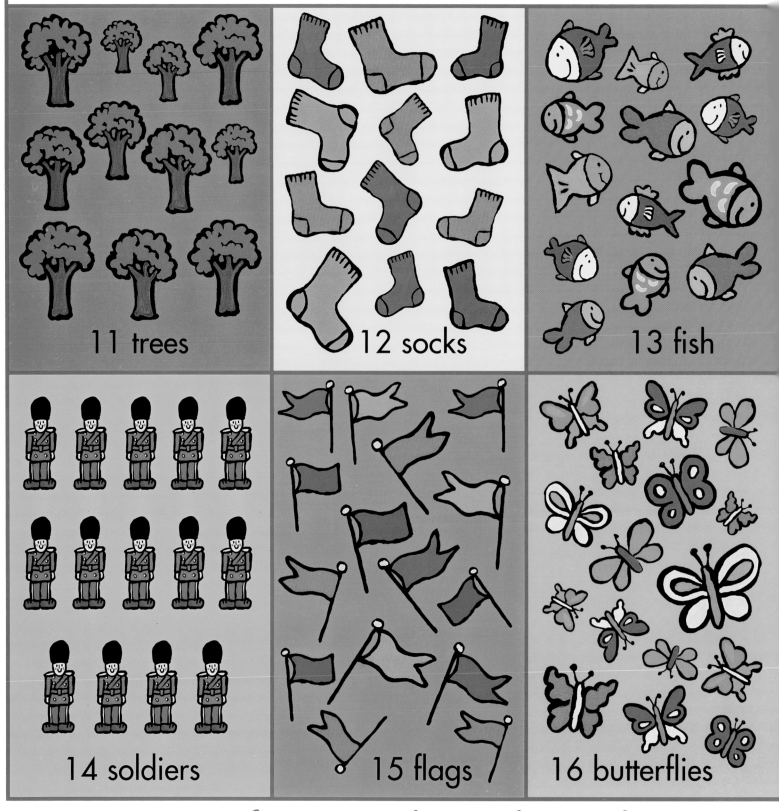

11 trees

12 socks

13 fish

14 soldiers

15 flags

16 butterflies

38

How many fingers and toes do you have?

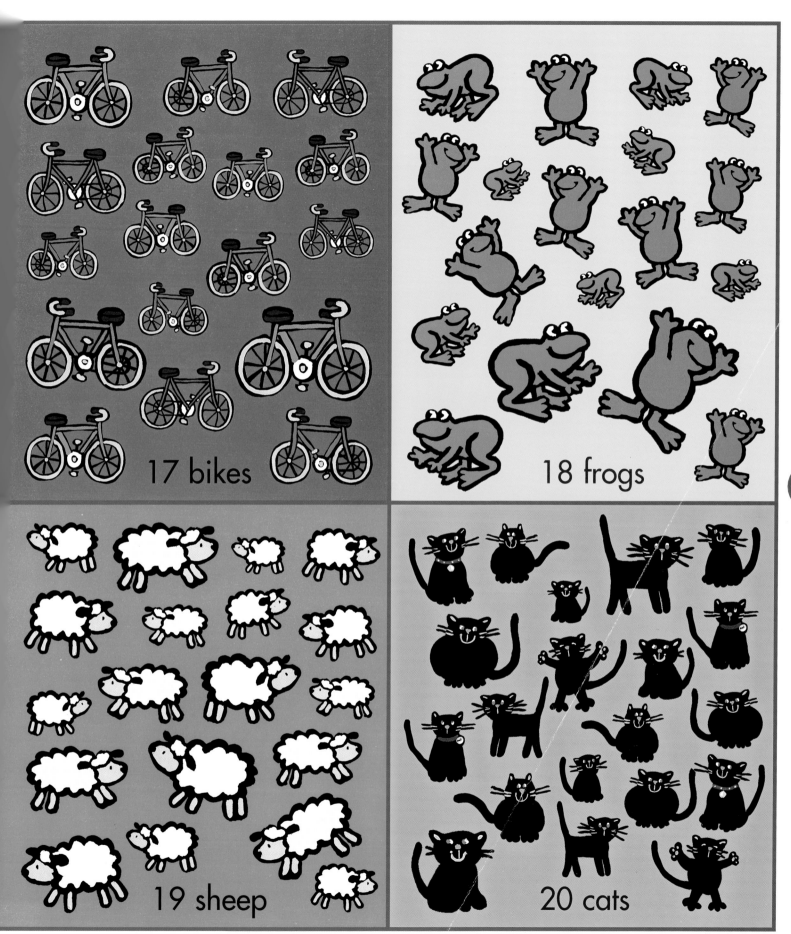

17 bikes

18 frogs

19 sheep

20 cats

Can you count 20 of anything else?

Can you find 15?

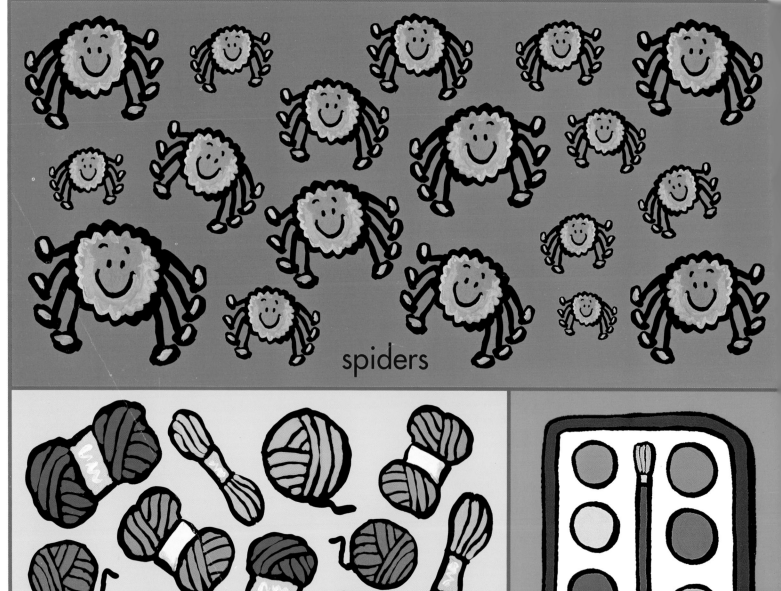

spiders

balls of wool

paint palette

Can you spot the number 15?

yo-yos

teddy bears

hot dogs

dragons

15

41

How many legs does each spider have?

Which numbers are missing?

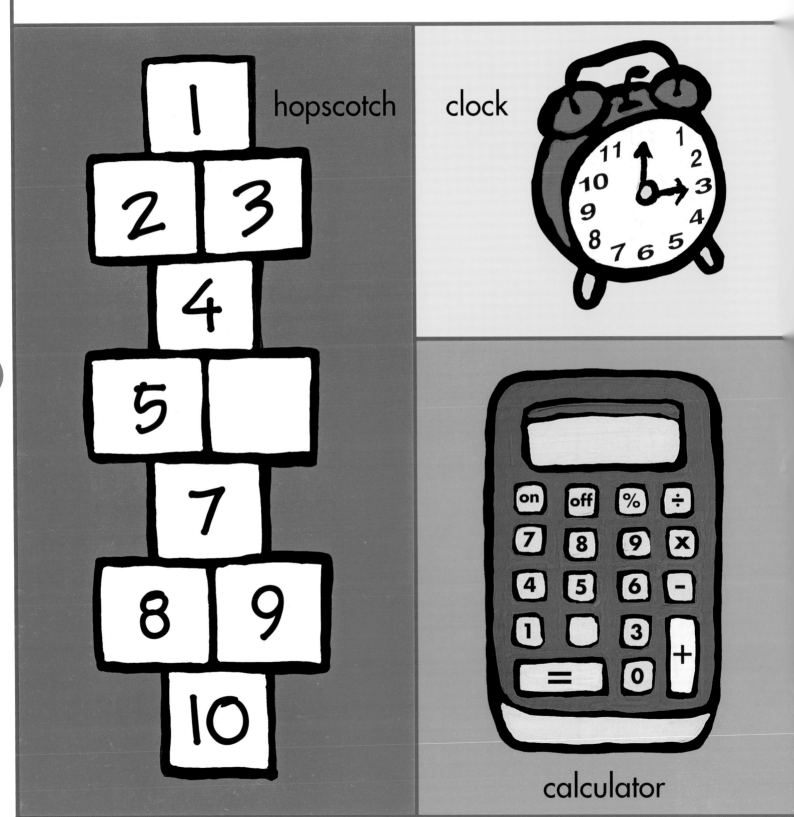

hopscotch

clock

calculator

Which of these numbers is the biggest?

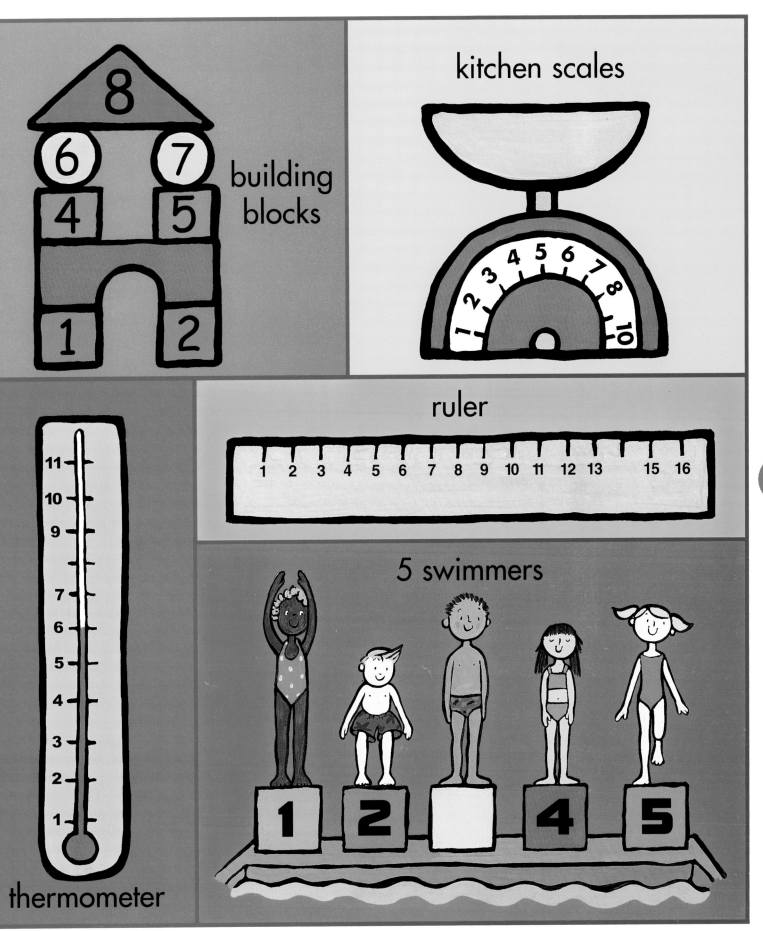

building blocks

kitchen scales

ruler

5 swimmers

thermometer

43

Do you know what time the clock is showing?

Can you count in pairs?

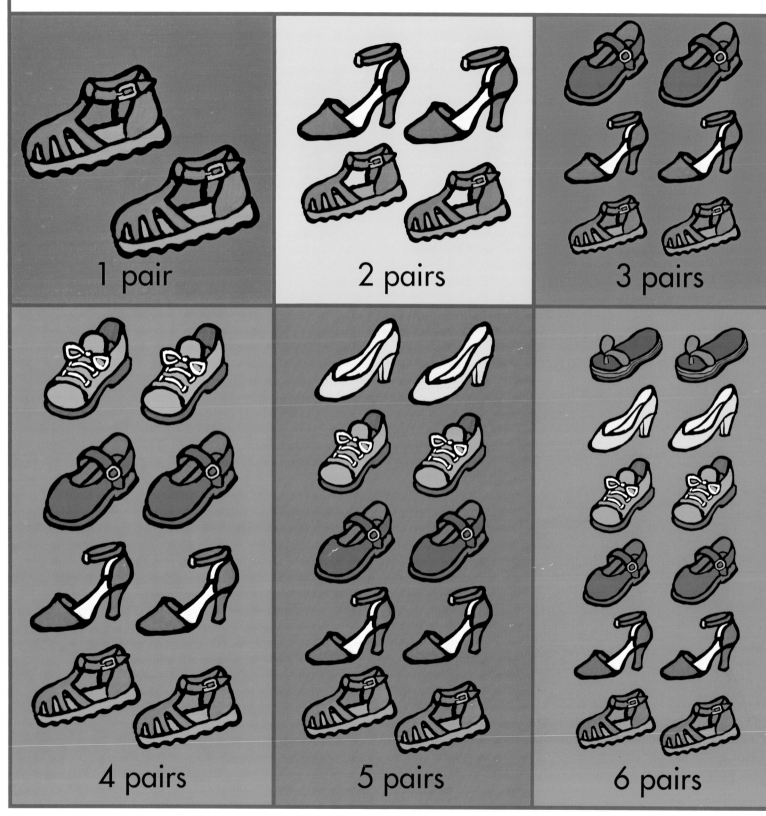

1 pair

2 pairs

3 pairs

4 pairs

5 pairs

6 pairs

How many pairs make 10 shoes?

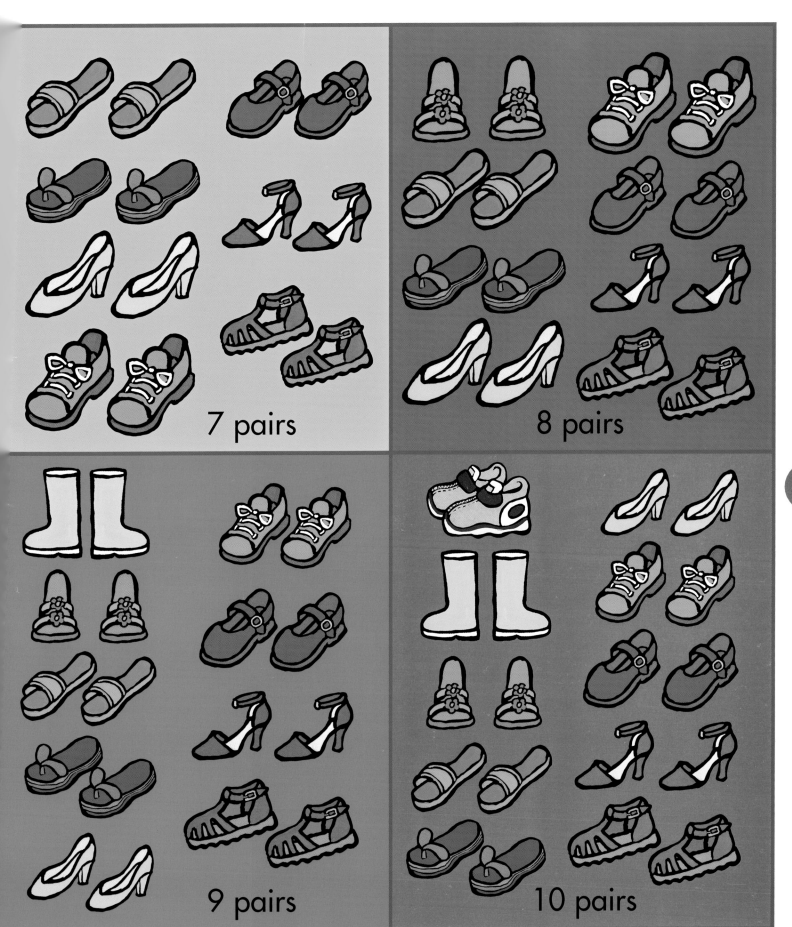

7 pairs

8 pairs

9 pairs

10 pairs

What other things come in pairs?

Find the numbers in the street

grocery stall

footballer

delivery van

car

What number is your house?

Seatown 12 km

sign post

61

bus

fire engine

gate

80

21

petrol tanker

43

petrol
pump

25·02
27·83 LITRES

Unleaded

What numbers can you see in your street?

Do you know these numbers?

0	zero
10	ten
20	twenty
30	thirty
40	forty
50	fifty
60	sixty
70	seventy
80	eighty
90	ninety
100	one hundred

500	five hundred
1000	one thousand
5000	five thousand
10 000	ten thousand
50 000	fifty thousand
100 000	one hundred thousand
500 000	five hundred thousand
1 000 000	one million